Poetry
in
Motion

DARRYL TINCHER

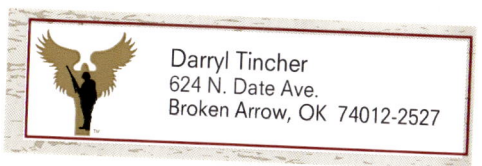

Copyright © 2018 Darryl Tincher
All rights reserved
First Edition

PAGE PUBLISHING, INC.
New York, NY

First originally published by Page Publishing, Inc. 2018

ISBN 978-1-64214-086-6 (Paperback)
ISBN 978-1-64214-085-9 (Digital)

Printed in the United States of America

Poetry in Motion

Spring, summer, winter, and fall
Every season has its purpose
Everything created for his glory
There is no life that is worthless

Seasons come and seasons go
God considers every heart
In his magnificent scheme of things
Every human has their part

Every sunset shows his glory
And beauty in every flower
The earth may shake and wind will blow
Reflecting of his power

The vast expanse known as "space"
God holds in the palm of his hand
Seven billion human souls
God knows every child of man

The sun, the stars, even the moon
Every wave of the ocean
The universe calls to Him
God's poetry in motion

Who Do You See?

When you look into his eyes
Who do you see?

I see a savior looking back at me
I see a king who soon will reign
I see a healer of hearts and pains
I see the son of a mighty God
The living truth though called a fraud
I see my Lord enthroned on high
I see a servant, the lamb of God crucified
I see the judge of all mankind
Appointed attorney our sins will he hide
I see God's love who came to earth
To give mankind a second birth

When I look into his eyes
Who do I see?

The hope of God to set us free

The Sower and the Seed

The sower sows the word of God
"But it doesn't make sense," some will say
And before the seed can take root
Satan steals it away

Some seeds fall on rocky soil
And with joy they spring to life
But when the trials come, they fail
Through the struggle and the strife

Some seeds fall on thorny ground
Their desire of "things" corrupt the heart
And when the seed starts producing fruit
It's choked from the very start

But some seeds fall on fertile ground
Cleared of stone and weed
Producing sixty and hundredfold
Continuing to spread the seed

The seed is life, hope and love
The great sower planted his son
So that many lives can reproduce
Because of the anointed one

My Father's Hands

These hands have mended fences
And taught me how to live
These hands have carried heavy weights
And showed me how to give

Callous from many burdened years
Providing day by day
My father's hands have always been there
This I'm honored to say

And though these hands taught discipline
And the commandments from above
These hands are full of tenderness,
Compassion, and God's love

Thank You, Mom

For buttons sewn, in stitch of time
For kissing cuts, to make them fine
For wisdom knowing, right from wrong
For all those happy birthday songs

For making lunch, I'm off to school
But you have taught the golden rule
For holding close, as storms go by
For answering endless questions "why"

But most of all, for who you are
For God has made, a shining star
To see the love, God has for us
So that one day, in him we'll trust

To Love and Beyond

God is love
Love is kind
Love brings peace
To heart and mind

Love is pure
Love is gold
A treasure to give
Not to hold

Love is patient
Love is strong
Quick to forgive
Every wrong

Love is like glue
It holds us together
No matter the color
We're birds of one feather

Love is everlasting
Beyond the grave
And in the end only love
Has the power to save

Walls and Bridges

The world has long been building walls
To keep the "unwanted" out
To find a path to a better life, they say
"You must find a different route"

Only the chosen, selected and few
Can enter into this place
Only the powerful, rich and strong
Are granted the privilege of grace

But we are all children of God
Created in his image you know
It's only by grace that we can stand
And only by love can we grow

He's in the job of building bridges
Where all can enter his place
For all who call on the name of Jesus
Will find amazing grace

Fully Restored

In a field, there lies a car
Forgotten were the days of old
When the car was strong
The days were good
But now for scrap is sold

It caught the eye of the restorer
Who didn't see just a heap
But a "diamond in the rough"
A classic that he would keep

Many hours of buffing and polish
The engine he had to rebuild
The master with love and patience
Had a promise to fulfill

You see, God loves the rejected
The humble and broken of heart
He promises to restore us
And give us a brand-new start

Instruments Astray

So many instruments
Playing their own song
Without a director
How could we know we were wrong?

Percussion was playing
Rat-tat-tat-tat
Woodwind was blowing
"You can't play like that"

Trumpets were blaring
We're the center of the show
We demand all the attention
As if you didn't know

Guitars were strumming
The violin screeched high
Then suddenly the master...
Director arrived

He said, "One instrument
Does not a band make
to play as individuals
Would be a mistake"

"All is noise
Like a musical haze.
Only together can you
Harmonize in praise"

"Play your own music
And all will go wrong.
For everyone desires
To play their own song."

"Play the music I give you
And you will see,
All will work together,
In harmony."

King of Kings, Son of Love

What should I say of the king of kings?
Rejected by the sons of men
We know him as the son of righteousness
Yet he carried the burden of our sin

Sitting on his throne in heaven's splendor
He noticed our struggle from above
Stepping down from his throne, he became a child
This son of God, son of love

The mighty king was humble
His love had brought him here
To conquer sin, death and hell
And deliver us from our fear

He united our kingdoms once again
This son of God and son of man
He's gone to prepare a place for us
To be with God once again

Rainbows and Storms

We love the sunny days in our lives
When everything seems to go right
And all the pieces just fall in place
There is no struggle or fight

But God's glory is only seen in the struggle
And when the storms come our way
For then his power is seen in the battle
And help is sent when we pray

In a blue sky the colors are not visible
So much of his glory we would not know
In nature's fury the colors are divided
And we see his glory in the rainbow

He Is J.e.s.u.s

(j. Justice)
In righteousness he banished man,
From paradise, because of sin—
Then they blamed the devil for their faults,
But corruption comes from within,

(e. Everlasting father)
The love of a father is a powerful force,
He desired to redeem his fallen man,
But man cannot stand in the presence of God,
Heaven came to earth to reveal his plan,

(s. Son of God)
The son of God came to reflect the father,
In power, in word, and in deed,
Conviction came in his overwhelming love,
Forgiveness was his creed.

(u. Unconditional love)
To establish a covenant with fallen man,
He must become the Lamb of God
And hold His power of defense,
Even when named a fraud,

(s. Savior)
He defeated death/he defeated hell,
Through the humbling of the cross
In losing all as a sacrifice,
He gained all through saving the lost

The Gifts of God

His name is Emmanuel "God with us"
But he did not come to be king
He did not demand taxes of his people
But the gifts of God did he bring

The gift of love was proven on the cross
The gift of life when he was risen
The gift of hope "I go to prepare a place"
He has freed us from hell's prison

The gift of peace in which he is prince
Of righteousness through faith in him
Of the Holy Spirit to give us power
To overcome the struggle within

Freely we have received, freely give
That is the message he gave
Not that we hold these gifts to ourselves
But that through us the world might be saved!

Darryl Tincher

From One Righteous Seed

When man could not reach heaven, heaven came to earth	The son of God, the gift to man, became a human birth.	To bear the weight of the world, although he never sinned.
Who could know, eternal life is what he held within?	The "seed" had died to bring forth life, but he conquered death and hell.	So all who believe in his name, forever with him dwell.

This Land Called "Egypt"

We were all born into slavery
So we prayed to God for deliverance
Then he came and saved us
Yet in our hearts there is little difference

For our hearts still remember Egypt
And our flesh desires her ways
We say we want to honor God
But our selfish desires are heard when we pray

So he takes us out into the desert
And we complain when times get tough
He feeds us with mana from heaven
But we say "it is not enough"

And when he told us to possess the land
Our hearts melted in fear
We see the task before us
And forget that God is near

So many are stuck in the desert
Never reaching the promised land
We still see ourselves as slaves at heart
So we continue pounding the sand

The world around us is Egypt of old
And we've been delivered from death
But as long as our hearts are on worldly ways
We can never enter his rest

Time

Time is a gift
That cannot be exchanged
It cannot be borrowed
Only rearranged

Time goes forward
And never looks back
Which is a quality
We often lack

It seems fast, sometimes slow
Sometimes completely lost
But all the wealth of the world
Cannot pay its cost

We often feel we're in its grip
Like a train going downhill
We want the power to change our life
And direct it as we will

But time is in the father's hand
A destiny awaits us all
To spend our time praising God
Or lose it in our fall

We have only one life to live
Be careful how you spend
It is an investment for this world
And the next life without end

The Humble of Heart

If you look at this man from his beginning
Born in a manger stall
Not a palace or a hospital
But the humblest place of all

You could not imagine the king of kings
Laying in the hay
You could not imagine shepherds and kings
Kneeling down to pray

For God uses the simple, humble and meek
The common to confound the wise
He looks at the heart of the hidden man
He does not judge with his eyes

The power of God is not entrusted
To the boastful, mighty and strong
He empowers the humble as children of God
For it is in him we all belong

Christmas Is...

The world sees Christmas
As snow on the ground
Evergreen trees
And that jingling sound

But what of Christmas
Without any snow?
Would that be Christmas—
And how would they know?

Then I think of Christmas
Years gone past
The love and the joy
We hoped that would last

I cannot remember
The toys long ago
And many a Christmas
Has come without snow

But the memories of people
With love in their hearts
Is a treasure that's lasting
And a joy that will not part

It began with a child
God's perfect Christmas plan
To deliver his love
In the form of a man
Now Christmas is a gift
That keeps on giving
As long as God's love in
Our hearts is still living

Thanksgiving List

When I was young I was asked
"what would you like on your Christmas list?"
And I could count the toys on my toes
And every finger on my fist

As I've grown older the toys are all gone
And I've realized there are greater gifts
No longer do I ask for toys
But I do have a Thanksgiving list

I'm thankful for the peace of mind
God gives me everyday
I'm thankful for his patience
He hears me when I pray

He strengthens me when I am weak
I am not alone
Empowered by a mighty God
Who sits upon his throne

All these gifts were secure
Two thousand years ago
His greatest gift is his love
He came that the world would know

Peace Not Piece

As human beings we often bring strife
Strife with God and man
Our words are masked with little white lies
Our good deeds cover our sleight of hand

Trying to gain a piece of this world
As much as we can get
We aim for the mark of success in man's eyes
As far as blessings we rarely make a hit

A piece of this world will never bring peace
It only robs our very soul
The treasures of heaven are the blessings we keep
When the peace of God we know

Reflections of His Glory

No one can gaze into his glory
At least not as mortal man
One day we'll put on immortal bodies
And then we can

Until then we can see his reflection
In the sun the flowers and the trees
His beauty is painted all over the earth
It proves he cares for me

For all things were created by him
The enormous and the small
All things were created for his glory
For the good Lord created them all

New Beginnings

New year brings a new beginning
The old year past the new to come
So many things of old year past
Leave us jobs undone

Convictions come by mistakes we've made
And regrets of things we've said
We make a vow to change our ways
But the same mistakes bring us dread

Only by grace can we change our ways
Only through love can we mend
For the grace of God is quick to forgive
So our new year can begin

My Father's Many Suits

My father has many suits
Some I do not desire
Like a constable who sets a curfew
And catches me in the midnight hour

Like a teacher he says
"You must do your homework
You cannot learn
Unless you open the book"

But he's also my coach
In this "game of life"
When I want to give up
Through all the struggle and strife

He teaches my hands
To do God's will
To seek for my purpose
And my calling to fulfill

And sometimes a hug
That's all I will ask
When I've failed to perform
And I've failed at the task

"Never give up" he says,
"We'll overcome
I'm always your Father
You're always my son"

(My heavenly father)

The Soil of Our Hearts

Not every seed can produce life
For it may fall on rocky ground
It springs forth in spring rain
But by summers heat it can't be found

The heart like soil can produce life
When God plants his seeds of love
And these seeds bring eternal fruit
Because they come from God's garden above

But when our hearts are full of stones
Unforgiveness and selfish desires
They will not survive man's ambitions
Or when we are tried by fire

Love is a seed that anchors deep
And survives through summer's drought
And when harvest time finally comes
We will find we've never been without

Come as a Child

Mighty conqueror king of kings
Lord of Lords is he
Rock of ages the holy one
But that's not how he came for me

To conquer our hate he came as love
To conquer fear he came as peace
Though strong and mighty he was meek and small
All my bondage now sweet release

Born in a manger the son of God
What gift would be worthy to bring?
The gift of ourselves just as he came
Come as a child before the king

Luke 18:15–17

Love and Righteousness

Love and righteousness worked hand in hand
When righteousness demanded a sacrifice
All seemed lost a hopeless cause
Until the righteous one paid the price

Some say there are many ways to heaven
But they have been sadly deceived
Jesus said "there's only one way to heaven"
And he's the one I believe

You see Jesus is love that is true
But Jesus is righteousness too
Both were proven on the cross
When he died for me and you

My Father's Shoes

My father's shoes are really big
I know I'll never fill
But he asks me daily to walk his path
And do my best to do his will

He's always quick to discipline
His children out of love
And his grace and mercy is poured out
On everyone from above

I seem to learn from the school of hard knocks
Even though his wisdom is plain to see
And when I admit he's right, I'm wrong
He smiles once again on me

Yes, my father's feet are really big
But I don't have to fill his shoes
As long as we walk in grace and mercy
And love is what we do

Vanity

In the mirror a reflection
As we perceive ourselves
Will others think us successful
As we gather our wealth?

We build great monuments
To honor our name
As we lust for power
Fortune and fame

But it's not enough
Our hunger is great
As we take from others
We seal our own fate

For life is not in taking
But it's given from above
It cannot grow in selfishness
But only in love

The life that we hold back
Is lost in vain
But the life that is given
Is born again

The Broken Compass

I had a broken compass
I knew not which way to go
Guided by the wisdom of man
How foolish! How could I have known?

To seek the things of this world
To fill this empty heart
Yet to have all the gold in the world
Without wisdom, it would depart

When I sought the wisdom of the Lord
My compass began to be true
The knowledge and wisdom to succeed
Is Gods spirit inside of you

Love as a Child

Joy and peace, life secure
Always wear a smile
Kisses and hugs, love burns bright
Faith just like a child

When I was young, life was new
My eyes opened wide to see
Now I'm old, life can be hard
What happened to the child I used to be

It's true I've matured and hardened with time
My faith sometimes grows cold
But don't weaken to a world of selfish gain
Hold on to a love that's bold

Pennies from Heaven

It used to be that pennies had value
And pop bottles were worth a dime
Now both are just thrown away
Signs of changing times

The blessings of God are pennies from heaven
The simple things of life day by day
The birds that sing, the sun that shines
And friends that come our way

Tossed aside in our busy world
Traded for all the "bling"
And in the end we've missed our blessings
That pennies from heaven can bring

Sowing and Reaping

I've heard it said
That we sow and we reap
But we cannot be blessed
By the seeds that we keep

And if we sow seeds
Of division and discord
Then a curse will be bought
As our reward

If we sow seeds
Of envy and pride
Than darkness will grow
From the sin held inside

But if we sow seeds
From the fruit from above
Then peace and joy
Will grow from his love

All God's Children

My God is a master builder
All things are in his hands
Nothing can surprise him
For he holds the master plan

Before he created the heavens
Before he created the earth
Before the first living thing
Was ever given birth

He knew that I would call his name
To redeem me from the grave
He knew that he would give his son
For my eternal life to save

He considered the cost from the beginning
Our journey and our fall
In justice we deserve condemnation
But in love he forgave us all

Before the World Began, He Knew

Before the world began you knew my name
You appointed a mission and a call
It has not changed although we fail
We stumble and we fall

Before the world began you knew we'd fail
You knew this from the start
You planned a way to save our souls
By sacrificing one pure heart

Before a builder builds a house
He considers every cost
And though the cost was very high
It was worth the saving of the lost

(Luke 14:28–29)

My Part for God

To each of us God has given
Gifts and abilities
We cannot reach our full potential
Until it is God not us we please

Not all are called to pastor
Not all are called to heal
But all are called to reflect his grace
We're empowered to do his will

Some may build some may paint
But all will light the way
Some wear suits some coveralls
But all must learn to say

"God has called me to do his will
Whether great or small
I'm part of his master plan to offer
Eternal life to all!"

Seasons of Life

Grass is green the color of life
Whose yards we proudly display
But life isn't easy with weeds to pull
And mowing the price we pay

Some have said "a gravel yard
I would never have to mow"
But tending the ground is a calling from God
As we watch nature grow

Like summer's heat and winter's cold
Are the cycles of a human soul
Without the testing of our lives
The grace of God we would not know

We may plant and till the ground
But it is God who gives life's breath
For he alone holds the cycles of life
And the power of life over death

Saved from Fear

Why is Christmas
Only one day a year?
When in all the others
Most live in fear

Fear of rejection
When God accepts us all
The mighty, the weak,
The short and the tall

Fear of lack
When we hunger for more
But there is no end
To God's heavenly store

Fear of death
And the end of all things
To know the prince of peace
And the life that he brings

When we know Gods love
And the price that he paid
From death, rejection,
And fear are we saved

All-Consuming Fire

Who can stand in the glory of his splendor
When he comes to show his power?
When all the earth will be judged
In man's final hour

For flesh and blood were condemned from Eden
When our pride caused us to sin
And only through the blood of Christ
Can we be cleansed once again

So when we stand in the presence of God
And mortal puts on immortality
This flesh will be done away with
And we will finally be free

(Isaiah 33:13-17 and 10:17-18) (Jeremiah 14:12)

Good News

I read the paper the other day
Hoping for good news
I saw skyrocketing gas prices
And Fox Collision singing the blues

War in the middle east
Taxes going up
A man lost his life today
In a collision with a truck

Why is there so much bad news today?
Because gossip has many friends
You didn't hear that a life was saved
Or that a couple is making amends

Hope is born every day
When we stop looking for strife
And look for the good in one another
To spread the seeds of life

Destiny

In the back of the book as the message goes
We live in perilous times
The daily news and cost of living
Weigh heavy on heart and mind

It's not with intellect nor physical strength
Not with wealth can we overcome
But there is a race an appointment with time
And a destiny we all must run

He came as a child humble and meek
Our burden he must carry
The path is before us for all who will follow
Our destiny through his victory

The Gift of Christmas

What is it of Christmas
That holds our hearts so dear?
Why is it this time of year
We hold our loved ones near?

We reminisce of days gone by
Of Christmases past
When all the gifts have come and gone
There's only one that lasts

The gift of Christmas warm and bright
Is like a shining star
Drawing on the hearts of man
The wise men traveled far

Born in a humble manger
A gift from God above
The only hope to change the world
The gift of Christmas is love

Friend of God

Some serve God in fear of his wrath
Attempting to escape the eternal flame
Preaching vengeance of an awesome God
Never shaking a servant's shame

Some serve as a wanting child
Never content with worldly things
Unable to see beyond the flesh
To share the gifts that heaven brings

And some serve God out of internal fire
The kind that's devoted to the end
Not just serving out of selfish gain
The kind of man God calls a friend

I want to be a friend of God
Reaching to the world from love within
Able to see through the eyes of God
Through the blood that washes every sin

Love's Light of Freedom

The people who walked in darkness
Have seen a great light
He shines now within us
Where no longer there is night

He came from a distance
He came from afar
Shining down from the father's heart
The son, the morning star

First seen by the wise men
Who longed to see the king
Then by the shepherds
Who heard the angels sing

He still shines over Bethlehem
For all the world to see
To break the chains of darkness
And set the captives free

In this Moment

Too many cares have caught my eye
Too many burdens pull me down
When I'm caught up in this daily grind
I forget that you're even around

Too many hopes and aspirations
Too many dreams to be fulfilled
I forget you are the strength I need
And for your purpose I must yield

Lord give me this moment to draw close to you
And remember each day is a gift from God
Give me this moment to see what life is about
Help me not to live my life a fraud

And remain forever in this moment

In His Kingdom

Light shatters darkness
Life defeats death
Faith conquers fear
And love is the way

Hope Was Born

If Jesus was born in December
As some traditions are told
Then he was born when death gripped the earth
And life seemed to be on hold

The only green was in evergreen
The wind howled a chilling blow
The ground no longer showing its life
But covered in winter's snow

Then a star shown over a quiet town
Where few had seen the light
The hope of life to be made new
An end to the dark of night

For life was born in a little child
And paradise we could find
For he is the door to heaven's gates
The hope of all mankind

A Journey of Thanksgiving

When the pilgrims journeyed to the promised land
They were really not prepared
They traveled in hopes of a better life
And their own spot of land "over there"

But their journey was hard and many died
Their hopes seemed buried with the snow
How could they survive in this strange land
For only God could know

The Lord had brought them an Indian scout
Who could speak English well
A man who had seen their native land
And could prepare them for this land where they dwell

When God has a promise, a plan for life
We may not know the way
He has already provided for the journey ahead
And he guides us when we pray

My Favorite Time of Year

This is my favorite time of year
Not because of turkey or toys
But seeing loved ones not seen for a year
And all the little girls and boys

It's easy to get caught up in worldly ways
Where gifts are seen as a measure of love
What I remember of Christmas yesterday
Is the joy God filled us from above

So hang some holly and mistletoe
Drink some eggnog too
But let's remember it's because of Jesus
He brought Christmas to me and you

The Outside Looking In

So many people looking for love
But it's a one-way road they find
Selling their souls to find a lover
Only to find themselves in a bind

So many people searching for peace
For a hope and joy that can't be found
They put their faith in worldly goods
With their feet on shaky ground

All good things come from the Lord
His blood has already conquered sin
But they'll never be found in their present state
On the outside looking in

A Wise Man's Journey

Long ago, in the east
A star shined over Bethlehem
Few had seen, and fewer followed
These truly were wise men

For they saw in the stars, A prophecy told
Of a child born to be king
Leaving home, they journeyed far
With the treasures they might bring

Could they have known, this child of God
Would reign in the hearts of men?
For only under his graceful reign
Could peace on earth begin.

There's Still a Savior

In a world torn by war and hate
It's easy to wonder if he's there
How can a God full of love and grace
Sit by and show he cares?

But God created man with a will
To choose to do right or wrong
Does a cold selfish heart guide our way
Or is love our hearts melody song?

God intervenes for the righteous' sake
That's why he sent his son
Some battles may seem that they are lost
But the war is already won

You may ask, "Is Jesus real?
Will hope for men endure?"
The answer is yes, he's in our heart
And yes, Virginia, there's still a savior!

A Love That Cannot Fail

The world sees love in flesh and blood
This kind of love won't last
Without the giving one to another
This love will fade like grass

Without the sun to bring it warmth
Without the nutrients to grow
Without the rain to quench its thirst
It dies beneath winter's snow

We need the son that ever shines
To guide us every day
We need the spirit's gentle rain
To fill us when we pray

But most of all beyond the flesh
Beyond a love so frail
We need the love of the father
A love that cannot fail

The Dowry

In the beginning God created man
Like a betrothed virgin the promise was made
To dwell with him in paradise
But a great price had to be paid

Once pure man became corrupt
For we had sold ourselves to sin
And we tried to find our way back to paradise
But the corruption was too great within

The Bridegroom saw that the bride had fallen
Her works had purchased the grave
But the Bridegroom's love would not give up
Only He had the power to save

His blood He shed to wash our sin
The dowry, with love was paid
One day soon the trumpet will sound
And He'll take his bride away

9-28-17

Not By Accident

It's not by accident that we are here
Third planet from the sun
Too far and we'd freeze to death
Too close, we'd be well done

All the elements came together
Water, air, and earth
No other planet we have known
Could give life its birth

The sun gives light, life, and warmth
And keeps death at bay
Holding us in our orbital path
Faithfully day by day

Such is God who lights our way
Who meets our every need
Guiding us in our path of life
For we are blessed indeed!

Love Presses On

I thought that I could overcome
All things with stubbornness of mind
Determined to overcome all things
And enemies of all kinds

But the challenge was relentless
And I began to lose heart
By will alone I was destined to fail
Doomed from the very start

What is this power to endure all things
When might seems to fail?
What is the light at the end of the tunnel
That draws us to prevail?

The greatest challenge was that of the cross
Burdened by the chosen one
When all else fails under the load
Love presses on

From God: To You

I awoke on Christmas morning
And looked under the tree
I saw many gifts galore
And some were meant for me

Yet forgotten were the gifts of past
Those toys have lost their gleam
The things that man has made will pass
And that joy was gone it seemed

Then I saw the gifts of God
Joy, peace, and love
Strength and overcoming faith
These gifts from God above

I awoke on Christmas morning
And looked under the tree
I'm thankful for the gifts of God
That he has given me

The Test of Father Time

This is a test . . .
This is only a test
And how we spend these hundred years
Determines how we will live all the rest

Chasing all the things in this life
What do we think we will find?
When we think we've found the best of life
In the end we'll find that we were blind

Love is life's purpose
When we learn to give
Sharing of ourselves
We learn to live

Seeing with love
Our eyes are finally open
Love has the power
To heal the broken

What is the meaning of life?
You may say
It's easy—we're here to learn
To love God's way

Will you pass the test?
Or will you fail
I guess it's true
That only time will tell

My Prayer of Thanksgiving

Thank you, Father
For I am abundantly blessed
I have peace that passes understanding
In you I find rest

I have healing and wisdom
Prosperity and love
The greatest of gifts
Always come from above

And no matter what comes
I can always say
"God's got a plan
You will see me through the day"

The Great Exchange

I looked for a king.
I saw a child
I looked for a conqueror
But he seemed mild

I looked for the strength to overcome
The weakness I saw in me
I looked for one invincible
Then he died upon a tree

I could not understand his ways
My life he would rearrange
My weakness he nailed to the cross
His strength I would exchange

I Am Blessed

I am blessed beyond what I can imagine
But I thank you for what I've seen
I've seen peace that passes understanding
I've seen great prosperity

And though this world has night and day
And darkness threatens to fall
The light overcomes the darkness
And shines when I call

Yes, my father provides for his children
And meets our needs day by day
I will praise my father always for
He hears me when I pray

Jesus Our Banner

King of righteousness, royal blue
Shed his blood for me and you
Washed our sins as white as snow
Now we are stars in heaven
(American Flag) Where we will go

Surrender

The very sound of it brings fear
Defeat, loss, bondage, failure
But only through Jesus can we find peace
When we lay down our pride and surrender

Surrender lofty dreams of fortune
Of selfish dreams of fame
Human glory can't live beyond this life
And there's power in only one name

In His Presence Is Peace and Joy

In his presence is peace and joy
There's no power in the grave
Only Jesus overcame the cross
And only Jesus has the power to save

The Proof Is in the Heart

All of creation shows his glory
And I have known his name
No book has been more printed
No name has gained as much fame

Yet man must reason in his mind
If there is a God where is his proof?
In all man's wisdom we've been deceived
Not knowing the lie from the truth

I've heard his voice in a quiet place
Felt his presence, my peace of mind
Seen the love humans can give
Through his grace we can be kind

Though my eyes have not seen him
And reason can't impart
I have no doubt of his presence
I have seen him in my heart

God's Gift of Gold

The world is full of glitter and gold
And treasures we might find
Entertainment seems to find its place
Within our hearts and minds

Driven by our own desires
And all that we can see
I've overlooked the still small voice
Speaking inside of me

God's gift of gold is eternal life
His treasure is peace of mind
That when all earthly things pass away
A home in heaven I will find

The Rest of Me

To the world we often show
Our good side and hide the rest
But to God we bring our corrupted side
And forget he wants our best

Not that he neglects our weaker side
He's making us better day by day
And when we don't know which way to go
He always shows us the way

So when you come to God, give thanks
And always bring your best
But don't try to hide what's broken from God
He also wants the rest

Human Host

Light and darkness seek a host
A body they can possess
With light we find eternal peace
With darkness there is no rest

Spirits need to express themselves
Light brings life and warmth
Darkness creates chaos
And all around creates a storm

Our hearts are a doorway to this world
Where life or death can be found
Darkness makes us hopeless
Light is a friend when no one is around

Children of light or children of darkness
Whose child will you be
One puts us in bondage
While the other sets us free

Stuff

What is this stuff that clutters our house
And clutters our hearts as well?
What is this stuff stacked to the ceiling
I'm sure it's beginning to smell?

What is this stuff that was once brand-new
And coveted by many a man?
Consuming our souls by desire of "things"
To the point that were ensnared by sin

Happiness cannot be bought with all the gold
Where heart is your treasure will be
Peace with God is worth much more
Only contentment in him can set you free

Faith, Hope, Love, and Peace

Faith is grown in a promise
Two thousand years ago
When the son of God came to earth
So that the father we might know

Hope is spread with God's word
He's our provider, healer and savior
No one can earn eternal life
For grace is unmerited favor

Love was proven on the cross
Innocent blood shed for our sin
Destroying the death that ruled our lives
That a new life might begin

Finally peace but not in the earth
It's our calm in the midst of the storm
For were in the presence of our God and father
Where he keeps us safe and warm

The Half-Empty Glass

The rain falls on the just and unjust
The sun shines on us all
The flowers bloom in the spring of our lives
And in autumn the leaves will fall

We are all tested by the nature of flesh
To trust in God at all times
To obey him when things have gone afoul
And to praise him when things are fine

The glass is half empty, the glass is half full
Life is a blessing to those who believe
That God in our emptiness will fill our need
Be at peace, and have faith to receive

Food For the Soul

In a vision I saw myself
Walking down a street
Hunger pangs driving me
To beg for something to eat

I stopped in front of a cafe
The people were smiling as they ate
But I hadn't a dime to my name
I was doomed to a hopeless fate

I turned to walk from this site
When I heard someone call my name
"Come here brother I know your hunger
And I have felt your pain"

The Door Man said "come in and dine
For all are welcome to feed
But it's not just food for your soul
It's eternal life you need"

"How can I pay? I haven't a dime
My burdon is too great within
But he said "don't you know the Master has come
And He's paid the price for your sin"

Why do we hunger for wordly things?
They leave us with an empty soul
The Master invites us to dine with Him
So that life and peace we will know

All in the Package

Healing, prosperity, forgiveness and peace
Power, love and joy
All delivered in a small package
In the shape of a little boy

The blind can see, the dead are raised
And the mute can be heard
The demons tremble at a little black book
The power of its spoken word

Though I am small in the world's eyes
And lack the wisdom of the ages
All things are possible to those who believe
Power often comes from small packages!

What We Leave Behind

In memory of Donald Tincher

When a good man gives his life
In service to the Lord
And provides for his family's needs
He is a light to family and friends
And he plants a righteous seed

No one knows the time that we have
Appointed by the father above
But in this short life that we live
The greatest inheritance we leave
Is God's love

Vows

Many vows are made and broken
Without considering the cost
We lose our focus on the goal
And our determination is lost

What is lacking is not desire
Nor hope for a good outcome
But the wisdom and guidance from above
Before the race is run

Consider the cost before you build
Make a plan to win
It's better not to make a vow
Than your mouth cause you to sin

Rejected Sacrifice

A certain king has a vast domain
And many provinces therein
He entrusted his vineyards to servants abroad
But alas—some have fallen to sin

"I'll send messengers to provinces near and far
To enquire their stewardship," he said
Some were beaten some were cursed some run out of town

Others ended up dead

"What a wicked nation that stands before me
They cannot know what they have done
They could not accept the messengers I've sent
Who could I send? I'll send my son."

The son went in love to spread the good news
That his father was a forgiving king.
Some accepted—some cursed him some even spread lies

In the end, the sting of death stung again

"My vengeance is against them for what they have done
I sent my son in forgiveness of their sins
But if they cannot accept him for such great sacrifice

Their lives I'll require of them

Miles of Heart

Life is a journey we all must take
Whether you ever leave your hometown
For life is measured in "miles of heart"
Not by distance on the ground

Across the street, down the road
People everywhere
A kiss, a hug, an encouraging word
Each one showing that you care

And in the end, our journey home met
By God's own son
We'll enter in our father's home
And hear him say "well done"

A Mother's Love

Creator of life through our mothers
Formed with his gentle hands
Lent to our mothers for a short time
In hopes to fulfill God's plan

But before we can take up our journey
A burden our mothers must carry
To show us the sacrifices of a giving heart
Which sometimes makes us weary

But it is love from the father up above
The giver of life itself
That shows us of a mother's love
One of life's greatest wealth

Thank you, mothers

The Heart of the Home

Mothers are a gift from God
From whom we all can learn
Their wisdom and their grace to teach
We're never too old to learn

Home is where the heart is
And a mother is the heart of the home
We'll always remember a mother's love
No matter how far we roam

God's Love through a Mother

None of the lessons in life are as important
As to learn the character of my heavenly father
And though my dad shows strength and courage
The greater things I learned from my mother

For how could I learn about sacrifice
And the price paid on the cross
A mother is willing to make many sacrifices
My gain was often her loss

You never heard of a father bear
It's the mother willing to lay down her life
And when there's sibling rivalry
It's the mother who brings peace to the strife

Teaching wisdom and the ABCs of life
Is not the job of the public school
And though a judge she shows compassion
Even when I am a fool

And when we grow up we may stray
But our hearts are never far from home
And though we travel this great wide world
We think of mom wherever we roam

Thank You, Mother

For every time you've wiped my tears
And strengthened me in the storm
For every time you've corrected me
From the day that I was formed

As a reflection of the Father's love
And grace you've shown to me
Your guidance through my walk in life
And molding me into what I should be

I thank you mother my childhood shelter
My sanctuary where I could stand
And now I see the strength in you
Was the grace of God's mighty hand

What Does the Lord Ask of Thee?

What does the Lord ask of thee
But a few simple things?
He is not a God whose joy is in wrath
But in the blessings he might bring

The world is full of guaranties
Of promises made to you
Many times they turn their backs
Only the Lord is faithful to follow through

There is no easy life to find
These burdens we must carry
God does not promise an easy way out
But through him I am strengthened when I'm weary

Sometimes the burden seems too great
When all prayers of hope have been said
I suddenly remember that unselfish sacrifice
Of our Lord, and the blood that he shed

What does the Lord ask of thee?
It's not so hard to do
Honor God—love God with all your heart
And love mankind as much as God loves you

Honor

Honor is faithful
To do what is right
To know when to yield
And to know when to fight

Between honor and pride
We're often confused
Pride can be selfish
And honor abused

Do what is honorable
No matter the cost
For when sacrifice is withheld
Honor is lost

The Fundamental Flaw

Sin is the issue but it's not our flaw
It's not what keeps us from God's favor
Forgiveness comes when we acknowledge sin
And acknowledge that there is a savior

But that's not the flaw its deeper than this
There's a deeper problem inside
A stubborn resistance that caused Satan's fall
The fundamental flaw is pride

Pride cannot admit when it is wrong
Will not yield to a righteous power
But love can overcome this human flaw
So that we are not condemned in the final hour

Don't Let Life Pass You By

Ever since I was young
People have had the same desire
After a hard day's work many complained
"I can't wait till I retire!"

They dream of vacations around the world
And travels to exotic places
Of Hollywood movie stars
And meeting famous faces

Wherever I'm at, I see God's handiwork
In nature and in people
Watching animals at the park
Or praising God under the steeple

Sometimes the simplest things bring joy
Why don't you give it a try?
Or you might find at the end of your journey
That life has passed you by

Beyond Face Value

In faces of people it's hard to see the heart
Or the pain that is hidden within
The weight of our daily life can be heavy
And the chains of a soul bound by sin

It's easy to react when someone speaks in half
And not see the cause of a troubled heart
Before we respond and open our mouths
Put on love and compassion from the start

Words to Think On

"Men are like steel. When they lose
Their temper, they lose their worth."
Chuck Norris

"Life seems to be divided into two
Periods in the first we indulge, in
Second we preach." Will Durant

"Draw a circle, not a heart around
The one you love, because a heart
Can be broken but a circle goes
On forever." Unknown

"No man can think clearly with
Clenched fists." George Nathan

"If people are good only because
They fear punishment, and hope for
Reward, then we are sorry lot
Indeed." Albert Einstein

No Longer Stranded

I was going down the highway of life
Looking for my own "thing"
Thinking I was invincible
With my own song to sing

One by one it fell apart
Until I was stranded on the side of the road
The tires had already gone flat
Too much weight from my burden and load

911 would do no good
I'm stranded too far away
No one could help me down this road
So all I could do was pray

I hear a voice say "be still my son
My arms can reach where you are
And when your back on this road of life
This time, follow my son, my star"

Living Waters

I found a place of living water
Its fountain is not always sweet
But when I'm sick or have a need
My problems he'll always meet

I found another well that tasted sweet
But was bitter to my soul
And when you drink of this well
Your problems seem to grow

The choice is yours, the word is true
Believe what you choose to believe
But if you drink from the wrong well
Your mind will be deceived

Holy Hole, Wholly Whole

Once I met the holy God
But my sin had put me to shame
For all the works I had done
Cannot compare to his glory and fame

The problem was I had a hole in my heart
I tried to fill with things
I had no idea the emptiness and sorrow
That worldly desire would bring

I had to yield wholly to God
Both my fears and my desires
Its then I felt a holy flame
A spark that set my heart on fire

Then my spirit was finally whole
The hole was filled in my heart
The holy one was wholly mine
And he promised he'll never depart

About the Author

God has a calling on everyone's life, and he has empowered us with the necessary gifts and talents to fulfill our calling. Poetry has always been in Darryl Tincher's heart. It has been dormant, but not dead. Darryl feels compelled to write the words that God has given him. It is his part. God's seeds sown through poetry in hopes of producing life, love, knowledge, and maybe conviction, to be more than what we think we are capable of. To be what God has designed us to be.

CPSIA information can be obtained
at www.ICGtesting.com
Printed in the USA
FSHW02n2211200818
51429FS